Piedmont Travel Guide 2025

Royal Palace,Bustling Piazza San Carlo,Rolling Vineyards, and Quaint Villages,Hiking In The Italian Alps With Map & Images.

Gladys J. Carron

Table of Contents

Chapter 1. Introduction

Welcome to Piedmont

I've always been drawn to Italy's rich history and breathtaking scenery, but Piedmont, with its hidden gems and true charm, has captured my heart. My initial visit was enlightening.

When I first arrived in Turin, I was enthralled with the sophisticated architecture and lively spirit of the city. While I was strolling through the Royal Palace, I was able to take in a glimpse of modern Italian life in the bustling Piazza San Carlo.

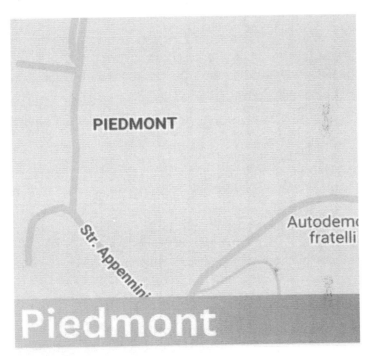

Scan the QR code

1. Open Camera: Launch your smartphone's camera app.
2. Position QR Code: Place the QR code within the camera's viewfinder.
3. Hold Steady: Keep the device steady for the camera to focus.
4. Wait for Scan: Wait for the code to be recognized.
5. Tap Notification: Follow the prompt to access the content.

Venturing into the countryside, I discovered the enchanting Langhe region. The air was filled with the alluring perfume of truffles, rolling vineyards, and quaint villages. Savouring the nuanced aromas of this renowned wine, I had a fantastic experience on a wine-tasting trip to Barolo.

One of my most memorable occasions was hiking in the Italian Alps. The sensation of peace, the crisp mountain air, and the stunning panorama were unmatched. I was greeted with expansive vistas that seemed forever when I arrived at the summit.

Piedmont's friendly and hospitable locals elevated my trip above and beyond the region's scenic natural features and historical landmarks. Their genuine friendliness and passion for their land were clear in every interaction.

If you're looking for an authentic Italian experience, Piedmont is the right destination. This area has much to offer everyone, from its mouthwatering cuisine and friendly welcome to its rich history and breathtaking scenery.

Reasons to Go to Piedmont

Piedmont, located in the northwestern region of Italy, provides an intriguing blend of history, culture, and natural beauty. This area, sometimes overlooked in favor of its more well-known competitors, has a certain appeal that will enchant you. Piedmont should be at the top of your list of places to visit.

A rich legacy of culture and history

Historical Cities: Discover the energetic, historically rich cities of Alba, Asti, and Turin. Each is home to several architectural wonders.

Discover the splendor of the Savoy dynasty's royal homes, such as Venaria Reale and the Royal Palace of Turin.

Ancient Villages: Discover lovely ancient villages like Barolo and La Morra, affording an insight into Piedmont's past.

Magnificent Natural Sceneries

Italian Alps: Take a hike or a bike ride through these breathtaking mountains to take in the expansive vistas and pure mountain air.

Lake Maggiore: Unwind on the shores of this lovely lake that is encircled by quaint villages and an abundance of flora.

Langhe and Monferrato: Explore the undulating hills of Langhe and Monferrato, famed for their wines and stunning landscapes.

Fine Dining and Wine

Piedmontese Cuisine: Savor the delectable flavors of this robust cuisine, which includes meats, pasta, and risotto.

Wine Region: Experience some of the best wines in the world as you explore the region's well-known wine districts, such as Barolo and Barbaresco.

Enjoy the excitement of truffle hunting in the Langhe region, which is home to a wealth of gastronomic delights.

Holidays and Customs

Wine Festivals: Throughout the year, several wine festivals will let you celebrate the rich wine culture of the area.

Local customs: Get fully immersed in Piedmontese customs, like the Festa della Madonna del Carmine and the Palio di Asti horse race.

Activities & Culture: Take advantage of Piedmont's cities and towns for classical music concerts, art exhibits, and other cultural activities.

A Synopsis of Piedmont's Cultural and Historical Background

Piedmont, a region tucked in northwestern Italy, possesses a rich and varied past that has molded its unique culture.

Historical Importance:

Celtic Origins: The region's history dates back to the Celtic Ligurians, who inhabited the area before the Roman occupation.

Roman Rule: Piedmont benefited from the infrastructure and cultural clout of the Roman Empire and was included in it as an essential aspect.

Medieval Period: Piedmont was split up into several principalities and duchies during this time, frequently stuck between the might of Germany and France's empires.

Savoyard Rule: The Duchy of Savoy and eventually the Kingdom of Sardinia-Piedmont were founded by the House of Savoy, which became the dominating force in the area.

Piedmont was instrumental in the unification of Italy, which resulted in the creation of the Kingdom of Italy with Turin as its capital.

Cultural Aspects:

Celtic Legacy: The place names, languages, and traditional trades of the area all bear witness to their Celtic origin.

Roman Influence: Piedmont's architecture, language, and judicial system are all influenced by the Romans.

Renaissance and Medieval Art: The cities of Piedmont, especially Turin, have a rich history of art, with many palaces, churches, and museums displaying pieces from the Renaissance and Medieval periods.

Savoyard Legacy: The architecture, traditions, and royal mansions of the area all bear the imprint of the Savoyard dynasty.

Alpine Traditions: The hilly areas of Piedmont have managed to hold onto their traditional Alpine ways of life, which include folk dancing, music, and food.

Piedmont's colorful culture is a result of its past, which combines Savoyard, Celtic, Roman, and medieval elements. For those who are interested in history and culture, the area is a fascinating destination because of its rich heritage, which is reflected in its art, architecture, cuisine, and traditions.

Chapter 2. A Look Around the Cities

Turin

Historical Sites

Antonelliana Mole

What to Explore

A famous skyscraper and museum in Turin, Italy, the Mole Antonelliana is recognizable for its unusual pyramid-shaped roof. What you can look into is this:

Panoramic views of Turin and the surrounding Alps can be obtained by climbing to the summit of the Mole.

Explore the history of film through interactive displays, historical relics, and screenings at the Museum of Cinema.

Elevator: Take an exciting journey in a glass elevator that provides panoramic views as it ascends to the top of the Mole.

Price

Panoramic views and museum entry are included in the Mole Antonelliana admission price. Seasons and any special exhibitions may have an impact on prices. To ensure you get the most recent price details, it is advised that you visit the official website.

How to Travel There

Conveniently situated in the center of Turin is the Mole Antonelliana. You can get there by:

Public Transportation: The Mole is accessible by foot from the "Porta Nuova" or "Torino Porta Nuova" bus or metro stop.

Scan the QR code
1. Open Camera: Launch your smartphone's camera app.
2. Position QR Code: Place the QR code within the camera's viewfinder.
3. Hold Steady: Keep the device steady for the camera to focus.
4. Wait for Scan: Wait for the code to be recognized.
5. Tap Notification: Follow the prompt to access the content.

Walking: It's simple to walk to the Mole if you're staying in the city center.

Hailing a taxi or using a ride-sharing service is a more straightforward and practical.

Extra Advice:

Get Your Tickets Online: If you want to avoid standing in line, think about getting your tickets online ahead of time.

Dress comfortably: Since you'll be walking and climbing stairs, wear comfy shoes.

Verify Opening Hours: Prior to visiting, make sure to check the website since Mole Antonelliana has specified opening hours.

Turin's Royal Palace

What to Explore

The beautiful Baroque building known as the Royal Building of Turin, or Palazzo Reale in Italian, was formerly the home of the House of Savoy. What you can look into is this:

Visit the opulently furnished royal suites, which include the Chapel, the Queen's Bedroom, and the Throne Room, to travel back in time.

Armory: Be amazed by the Savoyard dynasty's astounding array of weaponry and armor.

Library: Take a look at the vast library of the palace, which contains rare volumes and manuscripts.

Gardens: Take a stroll through the exquisite gardens of the palace, which include well-kept lawns, statues, and fountains.

Price

The fee Mfor admission to the Royal Palace of Turin varies based on the season and any special exhibitions. To ensure you get the most recent price details, it is advised that you visit the official website.

How to Travel There

The Royal Palace of Turin is easily accessible by public transportation and foot because I'mto its handy location in the city center. Here are a few choices:

Public Transportation: The palace is reachable on foot from the "Porta Nuova" or "Torino Porta Nuova" bus or metro stop.

Walking: The Royal Palace is conveniently accessible by foot if you are lodging in the city center.

Hailing a taxi or using a ride-sharing service is a more straightforward and practical choice.

Extra Advice:

Guided Tours: If you'd like to know more about the palace's history and architectural design, think about going on a guided tour.

Verify Opening Hours: Prior to your visit, make sure to check the website as the Royal Palace has defined opening hours.

Dress Appropriately: Since the palace is a formal venue, modest clothing is advised.

Realaria Venaria

Things to Look Into

Situated near Turin, Venaria Reale is a stunning Baroque castle and gardens that is recognized as a UNESCO World Heritage site. Here are a few of the standouts:

Explore the opulently furnished royal suites at the Royal Palace, which include the Queen's Bedroom and the Throne Room.

grounds: Take a leisurely stroll through the vast grounds that include sculptures, water features, and fountains.

Stable Courtyard: Take in the magnificent stable courtyard, built to house the regal equines.

Hunting Tower: Ascend to the summit of the tower for sweeping views of the gardens and castle.

The Museum of Hunting and Nature offers interactive exhibits that allow visitors to learn about the natural world and the history of hunting.

Price

The fee of admission to Venaria Reale varies based on the season and any special exhibitions. To ensure you get the most recent price details, it is advised that you visit the official website.

How to Travel There

About 7 kilometers (4.3 miles) to the north of Turin is Venaria Reale. The following are a few ways to get there:

Public transportation: Go to the "Lingotto" station on Turin Metro Line 1 and change to bus line 63. Take the "Venaria Reale" stop off the train.

Train: Travel to Venaria Reale station from Turin's Porta Nuova station by train.

Car: Driving a car can easily get you to Venaria Reale. The palace is close to a number of parking lots.

Extra Advice:

Guided Tours: If you'd like to understand more about Venaria Reale's history and architecture, you should think about going on a guided tour.

Verify Opening Hours: Prior to your visit, make sure to check the website as the palace and grounds have specified opening hours.

Consider a Full Day: Because Venaria Reale is a sizable complex, allot a full day to explore the gardens and palace.

Galleries and Museums

Egyptian Museum

Things to Look Into

One of the most significant museums dedicated to Egyptian archaeology outside of Egypt is the Egyptian Museum in Turin. Here are a few of the standouts:

View the preserved mummies of the pharaohs, queens, and priests of ancient Egypt.

Discover a sizable assortment of artifacts, including as tomb paintings, jewelry, statues, and papyri.

Explore the elaborate canopic jars that were used to preserve the deceased's internal organs.

Temple Reliefs: Take in the breathtaking representations of historical and mythical Egyptian subjects in the temple reliefs.

Price

The season and any special exhibitions affect how much it costs to enter the Egyptian Museum in Turin. To ensure you get the most recent price details, it is advised that you visit the official website.

How to Travel There

Conveniently situated in the center of Turin is the Egyptian Museum. The following are a few ways to get there:

Public Transportation: The museum can be reached on foot from the "Porta Nuova" or "Torino Porta Nuova" bus or metro stop.

Walking: You can get to the Egyptian Museum quickly if you're staying in the city center.

Hailing a taxi or using a ride-sharing service is a more straightforward and practical choice.

Extra Advice:

Guided Tours: If you'd like to know more about the background and objects on show, think considering joining a guided tour.

Verify Opening Hours: Prior to your visit, make sure to check the website as the museum has set hours of operation.

Because the Egyptian Museum is a sizable complex, allow time for a full day to spend viewing the displays.

Sabauda Gallery

Things to Look Into

A well-known museum of art in Turin, the Galleria Sabauda has an amazing collection of decorative arts, sculptures, and paintings. Here are a few of the standouts:

Italian Renaissance Art: Behold pieces created by well-known artists from the era, including Raphael, Titian, and Veronese.

Explore the masterworks of Flemish and Dutch artists, such as Rembrandt, Van Dyck, and Rubens.

Savoyard Portraits: Get an insight into the past and way of life of the Savoyard dynasty by perusing this collection of portraits of their members.

Admire the museum's exquisite collection of furniture, china, and tapestries, among other decorative arts.

Price

The season and any special exhibitions affect how much it costs to enter the Galleria Sabauda. To ensure you get the most recent price details, it is advised that you visit the official website.

How to Travel There

Conveniently situated in Turin's main center is the Galleria Sabauda. The following are a few ways to get there:

Public Transportation: The museum can be reached on foot from the "Porta Nuova" or "Torino Porta Nuova" bus or metro stop.

Walking: The Galleria Sabauda is conveniently located if you are lodging in the city center.

Hailing a taxi or using a ride-sharing service is a more straightforward and practical choice.

Extra Advice:

Guided Tours: If you'd like to know more about the Savoyard dynasty's past and the art collection, think considering joining a guided tour.

Verify Opening Hours: Prior to visiting, make sure to check the website since the Galleria Sabauda has defined opening hours.

Schedule a Full Day: Due to the museum's extensive art collection, allow enough time to explore the displays throughout the day.

Civic Art Museum

Things to Look Into

Large-scale Italian art from the Middle Ages to the Baroque era is housed in Turin's esteemed Civic Museum of Art, also known as Museo Civico d'Arte Antica. Here are a few of the standouts:

Explore the masterworks of Italian Renaissance and Medieval artists including Fra Angelico, Botticelli, and Raphael.

Baroque Art: Take in the vivid and dramatic paintings created by Baroque artists such as Bernini, Caravaggio, and Rubens.

Discover the sculptures in the museum's collection, which features pieces by well-known Italian sculptors including Michelangelo and Donatello.

Admire the museum's exquisite collection of furniture, pottery, and tapestries, among other decorative arts.

Price

The Civic Museum of Art's admission price changes according to the time of year and any special exhibitions. To ensure you get the most recent price details, it is advised that you visit the official website.

How to Travel There

Conveniently situated in Turin's city center is the Civic Museum of Art. The following are a few ways to get there:

Public Transportation: The museum can be reached on foot from the "Porta Nuova" or "Torino Porta Nuova" bus or metro stop.

Walking: The Civic Museum of Art is conveniently located if you are lodging in the city center.

Hailing a taxi or using a ride-sharing service is a more straightforward and practical choice.

Extra Advice:

Guided Tours: If you'd want to know more about the museum's past and its art collection, think considering joining a guided tour.

Verify Opening Hours: Prior to your visit, make sure to check the website as the museum has set hours of operation.

Schedule a Full Day: Due to the size of the Civic Museum of Art's collection, allow enough time to explore the displays throughout the day.

Purchasing and Eating

Purchasing:

Through Roma

One of Turin's most famous and sophisticated retail avenues is Via Roma. Encircled by elegant boutiques and historically significant buildings, it provides a great shopping experience. What you should know is as follows:

What to anticipate:

High-end boutiques: Here you can find labels like Louis Vuitton, Gucci, and Prada.

International Brands: Learn about well-known global brands including Nike, H&M, and Zara.

quaint Cafés and Restaurants: Take a leisurely stroll down the street to one of the many charming cafés or restaurants.

Historic Architecture: Take in the stunning design of the structures lining Via Roma.

How to Travel There:

Public transportation: Walk a short distance from the "Porta Nuova" or "Torino Porta Nuova" metro station.

Walking: You can probably get there on foot if you're staying in the city center.

Extra Advice:

Visit During Off-Peak Hours: If you want to avoid the crowds, try going to Via Roma in the early morning or late afternoon.

Arrange for a leisurely stroll: Via Roma is an excellent area to spend a leisurely afternoon because of its abundance of stores and cafés.

Take a Break: If you start to feel exhausted, visit one of the many eateries or cafés to relax and have a bite to eat.

Through Garibaldi

The picturesque pedestrian-only Via Garibaldi in Turin is well-known for its lively ambiance, hip stores, and mouth watering eateries. What you should know is as follows:

What to anticipate:

Boutique Shops: Find stylish and one-of-a-kind apparel, home goods, and accessories.

Cafés and Restaurants: Stop by one of the many cafés and restaurants on the street for a leisurely lunch or coffee.

Historic Structures: Take in the stunning architecture of the structures lining Via Garibaldi.

Street Performers: Take in the street performances and live music that happen frequently.

How to Travel There:

Public transportation: Walk a short distance from the "Porta Nuova" or "Torino Porta Nuova" metro station.

Walking: You can probably get there on foot if you're staying in the city center.

Extra Advice:

Visit throughout the Day: When the stores and cafés are open throughout the day, Via Garibaldi is very bustling.

Savor the Ambience: Allocate some time for a leisurely walk down the road and relish the lively ambiance.

Sample Local Specialties: Don't forget to sample some of the regional cuisine served in the eateries lining Via Garibaldi.

Dining

Eataly

For those who love food, Eataly Turin is a culinary paradise that provides a singular and immersive experience. Anyone who enjoys Italian food should make time to visit this expansive marketplace and food hall.

How to Travel There:

Public transportation: Go to Lingotto station on metro line 1. From there, Eataly—housed in the former Fiat Lingotto factory—is just a short stroll away.

Car: Parking is plentiful at Eataly, making driving a convenient choice.

Eataly Turin is guaranteed to excite your taste buds and give an unforgettable experience, regardless of your level of culinary expertise or curiosity about Italian food.

Piola

Real Piedmontese food is served at the well-known Piola restaurant franchise in Turin. Piola's wonderful food and welcoming setting make it an ideal spot to sample the regional flavors.

How to Travel There:

Turin is home to multiple Piola establishments. By using their online map or looking up locations on their website, you may locate the closest one. The majority of Piola restaurants are easily accessible by foot or public transportation because of their handy location in the heart of the city.

Alba

Things to Look Into

Alba is known as the World's White Truffle Capital and is a quaint town in Piedmont's Langhe region. What you can look into is this:

Truffle Hunting: Find these valuable mushrooms by going on a truffle hunting expedition with a local guide.

Truffle Market: From October to December, every Saturday and Sunday, the renowned Alba White Truffle Market is conducted.

Wine Tasting: Visit the neighboring wineries and taste fine wines such as Barbaresco and Barolo.

Wander around Alba's old center and take in the charming streets and medieval architecture.

Chocolate Shops: Visit the various chocolate shops in the area to indulge in delectable chocolate delicacies.

Price

Depending on the tour operator and the time of year, the price of wine tasting and truffle hunting may change. It's best to inquire with nearby tour operators for the most recent details on costs.

Scan the QR code

1. Open Camera: Launch your smartphone's camera app.
2. Position QR Code: Place the QR code within the camera's viewfinder.
3. Hold Steady: Keep the device steady for the camera to focus.
4. Wait for Scan: Wait for the code to be recognized.
5. Tap Notification: Follow the prompt to access the content.

How to Travel There

About 31 miles (50 kilometers) to the south of Turin is Alba. The following are a few ways to get there:

Train: From Turin's Porta Nuova station, take the train to Alba station.

Bus: There are numerous bus companies that run frequent routes between Alba and Turin.

Car: Driving to Alba is a simple task. The town center has a number of parking spots accessible.

Extra Advice:

Schedule Your Visit: Keep in mind that the White Truffle Market is only open from October through December, when truffles are in season.

Reserve Tours in Advance: It is advised to reserve wine tasting and truffle hunting excursions well in advance to guarantee availability, particularly during the busiest times of the year.

Dress Comfortably: Walking around the countryside is a common part of truffle hunting, so bring along comfy shoes and clothes.

Wine Tasting and Vineyards

Barolo

Italy's Langhe region produces the famous red wine Barolo. Piedmont is home to this region. One of the best wines in the world, Barolo is renowned for its nuanced tastes and lengthy age potential.

What to anticipate:

Wine Tasting: Discover the distinctive qualities of this renowned wine by sampling Barolo from different suppliers.

Vineyard Tours: Discover the terroir of the area and the winemaking process by visiting Barolo vineyards.

Wine Cellars: Sample mature Barolo wines and explore historically significant wine cellars.

Wine Festivals: Take part in Barolo-focused events and wine festivals.

Price

Barolo wine tours and tastings can range in price based on the producer and the kind of experience. To find out the most recent prices, it's best to contact nearby vineyards or tour companies.

How to Travel There

About 50 kilometers (31 miles) south of Turin, in the Langhe region, is where you'll find Barolo. The following are a few ways to get there:

Train: From the Porta Nuova station in Turin, take the train to Alba station. From there, take a bus or a taxi to Barolo.

Bus: There are numerous bus companies that run frequent routes between Barolo and Turin.

Vehicle: Getting to Barolo is simple by vehicle. The town center has a number of parking spots accessible.

Extra Advice:

Arrange Your Visit: September and October, when the wineries are available to guests, are the ideal months to visit Barolo for the wine harvest.

Reserve excursions in Advance: It is advised to reserve wine tasting excursions and vineyard visits in advance to guarantee availability, particularly during the busiest times of the year.

Wear Comfortable Clothes and Shoes: Since many vineyards are situated in rural areas, dress comfortably.

Barbaresco

Another well-known red wine from Piedmont, Italy's Langhe region is Barbaresco. Barbaresco is frequently compared to Barolo, yet it has distinct qualities and a distinct style all its own.

What to anticipate:

Wine Tasting: Savor the refined and nuanced tastes of Barbaresco from a variety of wineries.

Vineyard Tours: Discover the terroir of the area and the winemaking process by visiting Barbaresco vineyards.

Wine vaults: Sample aged Barbaresco wines and explore historically significant wine vaults.

Wine Festivals: Go to Barbaresco-focused events and wine festivals.

Price

Depending on the producer and the kind of experience, wine tastings and vineyard excursions in Barbaresco might cost different amounts. To find out the most recent prices, it's best to contact nearby vineyards or tour companies.

How to Travel There

Situated in the Langhe region, Barbaresco is roughly fifty kilometers (31 miles) south of Turin. The following are a few ways to get there:

Train: From the Porta Nuova station in Turin, take the train to Alba station. From there, take a bus or a taxi to Barbaresco.

Bus: There are numerous bus companies that run frequent routes between Barbaresco and Turin.

Car: Driving from Barbaresco is a breeze. The town center has a number of parking spots accessible.

Extra Advice:

Plan Your Visit: September and October, when the vineyards are available to guests, are the ideal months to visit Barbaresco for the wine harvest.

Reserve excursions in Advance: It is advised to reserve wine tasting excursions and vineyard visits in advance to guarantee availability, particularly during the busiest times of the year.

Wear Comfortable Clothes and Shoes: Since many vineyards are situated in rural areas, dress comfortably.

Gattinara

In Piedmont, Italy, there is a lesser-known but no less spectacular wine region called Gattinara. Gattinara, which is well-known for its robust and well-structured red wines, provides wine lovers with a singular and fulfilling experience.

What to anticipate:

Taste wines from Gattinara, which are sometimes characterized as having a "masculine" character with notes of minerality, spice, and black fruit.

Vineyard Tours: Discover the distinctive terroir and winemaking methods by visiting Gattinara vineyards.

Wine vaults: Sample mature Gattinara wines and explore historically significant wine vaults.

Wine Festivals: Go to Gattinara-focused events and wine festivals.

Price

Depending on the producer and the kind of experience, wine tastings and vineyard tours in Gattinara might have varying prices. To find out the most recent prices, it's best to contact nearby vineyards or tour companies.

How to Travel There

Situated in the Vercelli province, Gattinara is roughly sixty-two miles (one hundred kilometers) east of Turin. The following are a few ways to get there:

Train: From the Porta Nuova station in Turin, take the train to Vercelli station. From there, take a bus or a taxi to Gattinara.

Bus: There are numerous bus companies that run frequent routes between Gattinara and Turin.

Car: Driving to Gattinara is a simple task. The town center has a number of parking spots accessible.

Extra Advice:

Plan Your Visit: September and October, when the vineyards are available to guests, are the ideal months to visit Gattinara for the wine harvest.

Reserve excursions in Advance: It is advised to reserve wine tasting excursions and vineyard visits in advance to guarantee availability, particularly during the busiest times of the year.

Wear Comfortable Clothes and Shoes: Since many vineyards are situated in rural areas, dress comfortably.

regional cuisine

Bagna càuda

Bagna càuda: A traditional Piedmontese meal of vegetables served in a delicious sauce made with anchovies. A variety of raw vegetables, including carrots, celery, peppers, and radishes, are served with the sauce, which is traditionally prepared with anchovies, garlic, and olive oil and heated in a traditional terracotta pot known as a "bagna càuda".

Cost: Depending on the restaurant and the portion quantity, a bagna càuda dish's price can change. All things considered, though, it's a reasonably priced place to eat in Piedmont.

Tajarin al bianco tartufo

Tajarin al tartufo bianco is a rich pasta dish consisting of thin pasta (tajarin) made of eggs that is combined with a thick sauce of white truffle and butter. The creamy texture of the pasta and the subtle flavor of the white truffle combine to create a very decadent dish.

Cost: Since white truffles are rare and expensive, Tajarin al tartufo bianco is regarded as a posh dish. The quantity and grade of truffles utilized can have a big impact on the price.

Vitello tonnato

A traditional Italian appetizer called vitello tonnato is thinly sliced veal covered in a rich tuna sauce. The tuna sauce is made with cooked tuna, mayonnaise, anchovies, and lemon juice; the veal is usually cooked rare or medium-rare and served cold. This dish is elegant and tasty because of the rich, creamy sauce and the delicate veal.

Cost: Although the price of vitello tonnato varies based on the quality of the veal and the ingredients in the tuna sauce, it is typically thought to be an inexpensive appetizer option.

Al Barbera Risotto

Risotto al Barbera: A robust and aromatic risotto made with Arborio rice cooked in a savory broth flavored with Piedmont's full-bodied Barbera wine. Extra virgin olive oil and grated Parmesan cheese are frequently used to finish risotto. This recipe is rich and delicious because of the richness of the Parmesan cheese, the powerful taste of the Barbera wine, and the creamy rice.

Cost: Depending on the restaurant and the caliber of the ingredients used, the price of rigatto al barbera can change. Still, most people think it's a fairly priced main course option.

Vercelli

Gothic and Renaissance Styles

Nestled in the Piedmont area of Italy, Vercelli is a quaint city with a rich history that dates back to the Middle Ages. The city's extensive medieval architecture, which has been conserved, is a testament to its historical significance.

Important Medieval Sites:

Cathedral of Sant'Eusebio: This imposing cathedral, a masterwork of Romanesque and Gothic styles, is the focal point of Vercelli's medieval architecture. Admire its magnificent interior, high bell tower, and ornate facade.

Basilica of Sant'Andrea: The Basilica of Sant'Andrea is another striking example of a Romanesque church. It has a lovely cloister and a vault that holds Saint Andrew's remains.

Palazzo Comunale: During the Middle Ages, Vercelli's government was housed in this historic structure in the center of the city.

Discover the remains of this mediaeval stronghold, Castello dei Ravignani, which provides sweeping views of the city and the surrounding landscape.

Explore the ruins of Vercelli's mediaeval walls, which formerly served as defense against invaders.

Architectural Elements:

Romanesque Style: Round arches, thick walls, and elaborate carvings are some of the hallmarks of Romanesque architecture that can be seen in many of Vercelli's medieval structures.

Gothic Style: Gothic architectural features like pointed arches, stained glass windows, and towering spires are incorporated into certain structures, like the Cathedral of Sant'Eusebio.

Brickwork: One of the defining characteristics of the region's building style, elaborate brickwork patterns are frequently found in Vercelli's medieval architecture.

Rice Terraces and Food

Fields of Rice

Scan the QR code

1. Open Camera: Launch your smartphone's camera app.
2. Position QR Code: Place the QR code within the camera's viewfinder.
3. Hold Steady: Keep the device steady for the camera to focus.
4. Wait for Scan: Wait for the code to be recognized.
5. Tap Notification: Follow the prompt to access the content.

Baraggia Vercellese

35

In the Italian province of Piedmont, the large area of rice fields known as Baraggia Vercellese is situated. This distinctive environment is made up of lush rice terraces, complex irrigation systems, and flat areas.

How to Travel There:

Baraggia Vercellese is conveniently located for vehicle travel. Driving around the picturesque countryside and pausing at different overlooks to take in the expansive rice fields is the ideal way to see the area. To discover more about the agricultural history and culture of the area, you can also go on a bike ride or take a guided tour.

Extra Advice:

Visit During Rice Harvest Season: September and October, when the rice fields are at their most picturesque, are the ideal months to visit Baraggia Vercellese.

Savor Local Cuisine: Don't forget to sample the rice-based meals from the area, like panissa and risotto alla vercellese.

Take a Boat Tour: To get a close-up look at the rice fields, think about going on a boat tour through the irrigation channels. This will give you a unique perspective.

Po Valley

From the Adriatic Sea in the east to the Alps in the west, the Po Valley is a wide and rich plain that spans northern Italy. A place of great natural beauty and cultural significance, the Po Valley is well-known for its fertile agricultural land and varied ecosystems.

What to anticipate:

Explore the immense rice fields that cover most of the Po Valley, especially the provinces of Vercelli and Pavia.

River Po: Take pleasure in boat rides along Italy's longest river, the River Po, and take in the breathtaking scenery it offers.

Wildlife: Take note of the different bird, mammal, and reptile species that call the Po Valley home.

Historical Cities: Take a tour of the Po Valley's quaint historical cities, including as Verona, Milan, and Turin.

How to Travel There:

There are several highways, railroads, and airports that connect the Po Valley. The following are a few ways to get there:

Car: One easy method to get to the Po Valley is by the A1 motorway, which hugs the western edge of the valley.

Train: High-speed trains provide excellent connections between Turin, Milan, and Bologna, three of the Po Valley's major cities.

Aircraft: The Po Valley is served by a number of airports, including Verona Villafranca, Milan Linate, and Milan Malpensa.

Extra Advice:

Visit in the Spring or the Fall: When the weather is mild and the foliage is in bloom, the Po Valley is especially lovely in the spring and fall.

Discover Other Areas: The Po Valley is a sizable area with a variety of scenery and points of interest. Take your time exploring new places and finding undiscovered treasures.

Savor Local Cuisine: Take a look at the mouthwatering local fare, which includes a range of pasta dishes, fresh ingredients, and regional specialties.

Cuisine:

Tossed in the Vercelli

A traditional Piedmontese dish that exemplifies the region's culinary heritage is risotto alla Vercellese. Arborio rice, butter, Parmesan cheese, and a savory, rich broth flavored with vegetables and saffron come together to make this meal of creamy, aromatic rice. These components come together to make a supper that is both elegant and filling.

Cost: Depending on the restaurant and the caliber of the ingredients used, the price of Risotto alla Vercellese may change. Still, most people in Piedmont agree that it's a fairly priced main course option.

Acquerello Risotto

Risotto Acquerello is a gourmet rice variety that is highly regarded for its flavorful nutty taste, velvety texture, and remarkable flavor absorption. Risotto Acquerello is only one of the many risotto recipes that use it. Rich broth, butter, and Parmesan cheese are common ingredients used to make this opulent risotto. The end product is a rich, delicious, and creamy dish.

Cost: Risotto Acquerello is typically more expensive than other varieties of risotto because of the superior quality of Acquerello rice. Depending on the establishment and the particular ingredients used, the price may change. Nonetheless, it's frequently regarded as a wise investment for individuals looking for a genuinely remarkable eating experience.

Risotto con porcini mushrooms

A traditional Italian dish called risotto con funghi porcini highlights the earthy, deep flavor of porcini mushrooms. Arborio rice, butter, Parmesan cheese, and a tasty broth flavored with porcini mushrooms come together to make this velvety risotto. The meal gains a pleasing texture and a richness of taste from the mushrooms.

Cost: Depending on the season and the availability of porcini mushrooms, the price of risotto con funghi porcini may change. When porcini mushrooms are in season and the meal is at its best, it could be less expensive. However, because of the higher demand, prices may be higher during off-peak seasons or when porcini mushrooms are in short supply.

Sites of Religion

Rich in culture and history, Vercelli is home to several important religious sites that provide insight into the city's spiritual past. Below are a few of the most noteworthy:

Sant'Eusebio Cathedral:

The focal point of Vercelli's ecclesiastical landscape, this imposing cathedral showcases a fusion of Gothic and Romanesque architectural styles. It is a must-see because of its grand exterior, tall bell tower, and elaborate interior.

How to Get There: It is simple to walk to the Cathedral of Sant'Eusebio since it is situated right in the center of Vercelli.

Sant'Andrea Basilica:

The exquisite crypt and cloister of this Romanesque basilica are well-known for holding the remains of Saint Andrew. The beautiful architecture and calm ambiance of the basilica provide a tranquil haven.

How to Get There: The Cathedral of Sant'Eusebio is a short stroll from the Basilica of Sant'Andrea.

San Grato Sanctuary:

Located on a hilltop with a view of Vercelli, the Sanctuary of San Grato is a well-liked destination for pilgrims. The sanctuary is a wonderful location for a peaceful period of contemplation and provides expansive views of the city and the surrounding countryside.

How to Get There: From the city center, you can take a bus or drive to the Sanctuary of San Grato.

Synagogue for Jews:

The synagogue in Vercelli provides evidence of the Jewish community's long history and presence in the city. Offering guided tours, the synagogue is a stunning specimen of Moorish architecture.

How to Get There: It is simple to walk to the Jewish Synagogue from Vercelli's old center.

Extra Advice:

Dress Modestly: It's crucial to wear modest and polite clothing when attending places of worship.

41

Verify the Opening Hours: On weekends and holidays in particular, some religious institutions may have restricted hours.

Guided Tours: If you want to know more about the background and significance of these holy sites, think about joining a guided tour.

Asti

Wine Areas and Events

The quaint Italian city of Asti is well-known for its sparkling wines, especially Moscato d'Asti. Asti is located in Piedmont. This charming area has lively wineries, lively celebrations, and stunning vineyards.

Wine Area:

Moscato d'Asti

Italy's Asti area produces the well-known sparkling wine Moscato d'Asti. A popular option for aperitifs and celebrations, Moscato d'Asti is renowned for its sweet, flowery flavor and low alcohol level.

What to anticipate:

Sweet and Fruity Taste: Moscato d'Asti has a fruity aroma with hints of citrus, peach, and apricot. It also has a subtle sweetness.

Low Alcohol concentration: Moscato d'Asti is a light and delightful wine, with an average alcohol concentration of 5–5.5%.

Bubbles: Moscato d'Asti's sparkling quality contributes to its lively and joyous essence.

Scan the QR code
1. Open Camera: Launch your smartphone's camera app.
2. Position QR Code: Place the QR code within the camera's viewfinder.
3. Hold Steady: Keep the device steady for the camera to focus.
4. Wait for Scan: Wait for the code to be recognized.
5. Tap Notification: Follow the prompt to access the content.

How to Travel There:

One way to personally enjoy Moscato d'Asti is to travel to the Asti region in Piedmont, Italy. This is how to go there:

Train: From Turin's Porta Nuova station, take the train to Asti station.

Bus: Numerous bus companies run frequent routes between Asti and Turin.

Car: Driving a car to Asti is quite convenient. In the city center, there are multiple parking lots.

Extra Advice:

Visit During Harvest Season: To experience the lively environment and taste fresh, regional wines, September and October are the ideal months to visit Asti.

Investigate Vineyards: Asti region vineyards provide tours and tastings where you may experience several Moscato d'Asti varietals and gain knowledge about the winemaking process.

Match with Food: Moscato d'Asti goes nicely with a range of cuisines, such as sweets, light appetizers, and spicy meals.

Barbera d'Asti

Italy's Asti area produces the robust red wine known as Barbera d'Asti. Barbera d'Asti, renowned for its intense flavors and lively acidity, is a well-liked option for individuals who want robust wines with personality.

What to anticipate:

Strong tastes: Typically, Barbera d'Asti has strong tastes of spice, cherry, and plum. The sweetness is counterbalanced by a notable acidity.

Age-Worthy: Barbera d'Asti, even if it's young, may be appreciated right away. With time, it will gain depth and nuance.

Barbera d'Asti goes nicely with substantial foods like cheese, meat, and pasta.

How to Travel There:

In Piedmont, Italy, you can travel to the Asti region to personally experience Barbera d'Asti. This is how to go there:

Train: From Turin's Porta Nuova station, take the train to Asti station.

Bus: Numerous bus companies run frequent routes between Asti and Turin.

Car: Driving a car to Asti is quite convenient. In the city center, there are multiple parking lots.

Extra Advice:

Visit During Harvest Season: To experience the lively environment and taste fresh, regional wines, September and October are the ideal months to visit Asti.

Investigate Vineyards: Asti region vineyards provide tours and tastings where you may experience several Barbera d'Asti varietals and gain knowledge about the winemaking process.

Match with Food: Hearty foods like pasta, meat, and cheese go well with Barbera d'Asti.

Acquiring Brachetto

The Italian Piedmont region of Acqui Terme produces the sparkling red wine known as Brachetto d'Acqui. A favorite for festivals and aperitifs, Brachetto d'Acqui is well-known for its sweet, fruity flavor and vivid color.

What to anticipate:

Sweet and Fruity Taste: The perfume of Brachetto d'Acqui is fruity and delicate, with hints of strawberry, raspberry, and rose petals.

Low Alcohol concentration: Brachetto d'Acqui is a crisp and light wine, with an average alcohol concentration of 5–5.5%.

Bright Color: The unique ruby-red hue of this sparkling wine enhances its aesthetic appeal.

How to Travel There:

You can travel to the Acqui Terme area of Piedmont, Italy, to experience Brachetto d'Acqui. This is how to go there:

Train: Travel to Acqui Terme station from Turin Porta Nuova station via train.

Bus: Numerous bus companies run frequent routes between Acqui Terme and Turin.

Car: Driving to Acqui Terme is a simple task. In the city center, there are multiple parking lots.

Extra Advice:

Visit During Harvest Season: To experience the lively environment and taste fresh, regional wines, Acqui Terme is best visited in September and October, during the grape harvest season.

Visit Vineyards: A lot of the Acqui Terme region's vineyards provide tours and tastings so you can experience the many Brachetto d'Acqui varietals and learn about the winemaking process.

Brachetto d'Acqui goes nicely with a wide range of cuisines, such as sweets, savory entrees, and light appetizers.

Wine Events

The Wine Festival

When and Where:

Held in Asti, Piedmont, Italy, every year is the Festa dell'Uva or Grape Festival. Although the precise dates are different every year, it usually happens in October, which is when grapes are harvested.

What to anticipate:

Grape Harvest Parades: Take in vibrant parades with floats that are themed around grapes and ornamented with grapes.

Wine Tastings: Indulge in a selection of regional wines like as Brachetto d'Acqui, Barbera d'Asti, and Moscato d'Asti.

Experience the sounds and movements of traditional Piedmontese music and dance.

Food Stalls: Savor delectable regional fare, including meals prepared with grapes and other locally sourced products.

Watch the Festa dell'Uva Wine Queen get crowned at the Wine Queen Contest.

Price:

It costs nothing to attend the Festa dell'Uva, however, there may be fees for food, wine tastings, and other events.

How to Travel There:

About 50 kilometers (31 miles) south of Turin is where you'll find Asti. The following are a few ways to get there:

Train: From Turin's Porta Nuova station, take the train to Asti station.

Bus: Numerous bus companies run frequent routes between Asti and Turin.

Car: Driving a car to Asti is quite convenient. In the city center, there are multiple parking lots.

Extra Advice:

Arrange Your Visit: Due to the popularity of the Festa dell'Uva, it is advised that you make travel and lodging arrangements in advance.

Dress comfortably because the event will be held outside. Bring loose-fitting clothes and shoes.

Savor the Ambience: Give yourself over to the joyous mood and take in the lively enthusiasm of the attendees.

Festival of Asti Spumante

When and Where:

The Asti Spumante Festival normally takes place in April or May during the spring season. For the most recent details, it's advisable to visit the official website as the dates are subject to change every year. The event is held in Asti, an enchanting city in Italy's Piedmont region.

What to anticipate:

Wine Tastings: Try some of the sparkling wine known as Asti Spumante, which is the festival's namesake.

Attend wine seminars to hear from specialists about the origins and manufacturing process of Asti Spumante.

Cultural Events: Take in street shows, live music, and other artistic endeavors.

Food Stalls: Savor delectable regional fare, such as classic Piedmontese meals.

Price:

While admission to the Asti Spumante Festival is often free, there may be fees for wine tastings, food, and other events.

How to Travel There:

About 50 kilometers (31 miles) south of Turin is where you'll find Asti. The following are a few ways to get there:

Train: From Turin's Porta Nuova station, take the train to Asti station.

Bus: There are numerous bus companies that run frequent routes between Asti and Turin.

Car: Driving a car to Asti is quite convenient. In the city center, there are multiple parking lots.

Extra Advice:

Arrange Your Visit: Due to the popularity of the Asti Spumante Festival, it is advised that you make reservations for lodging and travel ahead of time.

Dress comfortably because the event will be held outside. Bring loose-fitting clothes and shoes.

Savor the Ambience: Bask in the joyous ambiance as you toast to Asti's sparkling wines.

d'Asti Barbera Festival

When and Where:

Usually taking place in September or October, the Barbera d'Asti Festival falls during the grape harvest season. For the most recent details, it's advisable to visit the official website as the dates are subject to change every year. The event is held in Asti, an enchanting city in Italy's Piedmont region.

What to anticipate:

Wine Tastings: Indulge in a range of Barbera d'Asti wines, a robust red wine renowned for its vivid acidity and strong flavors.

Attend wine seminars to hear from professionals about the origins and manufacture of Barbera d'Asti.

Cultural Events: Take in street shows, live music, and other artistic endeavors.

Food Stalls: Savor delectable regional fare, such as foods that go well with Barbera d'Asti.

Price:

While admission to the Barbera d'Asti Festival is normally free, there may be fees for food, wine tastings, and other events.

How to Travel There:

About 50 kilometers (31 miles) south of Turin is where you'll find Asti. The following are a few ways to get there:

Train: From Turin's Porta Nuova station, take the train to Asti station.

Bus: Numerous bus companies run frequent routes between Asti and Turin.

Car: Driving a car to Asti is quite convenient. In the city center, there are multiple parking lots.

Extra Advice:

Arrange Your Visit: Because the Barbera d'Asti Festival is a well-attended event, it is advised to make travel and lodging arrangements in advance.

Dress comfortably because the event will be held outside. Bring loose-fitting clothes and shoes.

Savor the Ambience: Take in the joyous surroundings and commemorate Asti's illustrious wine heritage.

Center of the Historic

Things to Look Into:

The picturesque labyrinth of piazzas, winding lanes, and ancient buildings makes up Asti's old center. Here are a few of the standouts:

Piazza del Duomo: This central plaza is home to the stunning Sant'Emerano Cathedral, a Romanesque structure.

Sant'Emerano Cathedral: Take in this magnificent cathedral's elaborate exterior and interior design.

Explore the Renaissance-style Palazzo Mazzetti, which is home to a decorative arts museum.

Torre dell'Orologio: Ascend to the summit of this clock tower for sweeping city views.

Piazza San Martino: Take a look at this quaint square, which is well-known for its energetic vibe and outside cafes.

Walking along this pedestrian-only route featuring stores, eateries, and historic buildings is called Via Alfieri.

Price:

Visits to the majority of the sights in Asti's historic center are free. However, some museums and guided excursions may charge an admission price.

How to Travel There:

About 50 kilometers (31 miles) south of Turin is where you'll find Asti. The following are a few ways to get there:

Train: From Turin's Porta Nuova station, take the train to Asti station.

Bus: There are numerous bus companies that run frequent routes between Asti and Turin.

Car: Driving a car to Asti is quite convenient. In the city center, there are multiple parking lots.

Extra Advice:

Get Lost in the Streets: It's best to explore the historic center on foot, so give yourself plenty of time to meander around the little alleyways in search of hidden treasures.

Savor Local Cuisine: Visit the numerous eateries and cafés in the old center to savor mouthwatering Piedmontese cuisine.

Visit During Festivals: Asti holds a number of festivals all year long, including as the Asti Spumante Festival and the Festa dell'Uva. The lively mood of the city is enhanced by these events.

regional customs

Piedmont has a tapestry of regional customs that uniquely capture the essence of the region thanks to its rich history and wide range of cultural influences. The following are a few of the more noteworthy customs:

Wine and Food:

Piedmont is known for its white truffles, and the pursuit of truffles is a highly valued custom. Take a truffle hunt with a knowledgeable local guide and enjoy the flavor and aroma of these highly sought-after mushrooms.

Wine Festivals: Throughout the year, a number of wine festivals, like the Barolo Wine Festival and the Barbera d'Asti Festival, provide visitors a chance to immerse themselves in the lively wine culture of Piedmont.

Piedmont is a hub for the Slow Food movement, which supports the preservation of regional producers and traditional foodways.

Festivals of Religion:

Turin's Festa della Madonna del Carmine is a religious celebration that includes vibrant processions, pyrotechnics, and traditional music.

Sagras: Piedmont is home to a number of sagras, or regional celebrations, honoring certain goods or saints. These celebrations frequently feature food vendors, live music, and dancing.

Cultural Occasions:

Every September, Asti hosts the Palio di Asti, a classic horse race that draws spectators from all across Italy.

Piedmont celebrates Carnival with traditional costumes, masked balls, and vibrant parades.

Fiera del Bue Grasso: This yearly event in Turin includes food vendors, rides, entertainment, and a contest for the biggest ox.

Dance and Music:

Piedmontese folk music: Take in the sounds of traditional Piedmontese music, accompanied by instruments such as tambourines, accordions, and bagpipes.

Piedmontese Dances: Get familiar with and enjoy classic Piedmontese dances, such the "tarantella" and "pizzica."

Arts & Traditions:

Knitting & Embroidery: Piedmont is renowned for its talented artisans who use needle and thread to make exquisite garments and textiles.

Ceramics: Learn about the area's pottery heritage, as stores and studios sell one-of-a-kind ceramic items.

Woodcarving: Take in the exquisite woodcarvings produced by Piedmont's talented artists.

These are but a handful of the numerous regional customs that contribute to Piedmont's rich cultural heritage. You can learn more about the history, culture, and way of life of the area by participating in these customs firsthand.

Chapter 3. Outdoor Experiences

Montego and Langhe

Trekking & Hiking

Langhe and Monferrato Hiking and Trekking: A Nature Lover's Paradise

Hiking and trekking are highly recommended in Piedmont, Italy's Langhe and Monferrato areas due to its breathtaking scenery, undulating hills, and charming vineyards. Here's what to anticipate:

Beautiful Trails:

Hiking Trail Barolo: This well-liked path gives stunning views of the Langhe hills as it winds through vineyards.

Monferrato Regional Park: Take in the park's varied scenery, which includes wineries, meadows, and woodlands.

Trails for Truffle Hunting: Take a guided trip and go through the forest to find these highly sought-after mushrooms.

Walks in Vineyards:

Wine Estate Trails: To learn about the winemaking process and take in the beautiful scenery, several wineries in the Langhe and Monferrato offer guided walks through their vineyards.

Levels of Difficulty:

Beginner-friendly: There are lots of easy-to-moderate treks that are appropriate for first-timers, such as strolls beside rivers and through vineyards.

Challenging paths: There are several challenging paths available for hikers with greater experience, offering possibilities to explore secluded locations, steep ascents, and panoramic vistas.

A Few Hints for Trekking and Hiking:

Put on the Right Shoes or Boots: To properly navigate the terrain, you must wear sturdy hiking shoes or boots.

Bring the necessities: a hat, drink, snacks, and sunscreen.

Verify the weather: Pay attention to the forecast and make plans appropriately.

Respect the Environment: To preserve the area's natural beauty, leave no trace and abide by local regulations.

How to Travel There:

You can fly into Genoa Cristoforo Colombo Airport or Turin International Airport to get to the Langhe and Monferrato districts. From there, you can go by bus or train to the adjacent cities of Alba or Asti, which are useful hubs for exploring the area.

Routes for Cycling

A cyclist's paradise with rolling hills, attractive vineyards, and quaint villages may be found in the Langhe and Monferrato districts. These are a few well-liked bicycle routes:

The Wine Route of Barolo:

Description: Offering breathtaking vistas of vineyards and old castles, this picturesque road goes through the Barolo wine area.

About thirty kilometers (19 miles) is the distance.

Moderate in difficulty

Route from Alba to Barbaresco:

This path passes past vineyards, olive orchards, and quaint villages as it winds through the heart of the Langhe area.

The distance is roughly twenty-five kilometers (16 miles).

Moderate in difficulty

Route Monferrato Hills:

Description: This strenuous route offers breathtaking panoramic vistas and endless vineyards as you explore the rolling hills of Monferrato.

Distance: Varies based on the selected path

Level of difficulty: Hard

How to Travel There:

You can fly into Genoa Cristoforo Colombo Airport or Turin International Airport to get to the Langhe and Monferrato districts. From there, you can go by bus or train to the adjacent cities of Alba or Asti, which are useful hubs for exploring the area.

Extra Advice:

Hire a Bike: The Langhe and Monferrato regions have several bike rental businesses that let you see the area at your own speed.

Plan Your Route: When deciding on a bike route, take your fitness level and available time into account.

Savor the Scenery: Stop along the journey to enjoy the breathtaking views of the vineyards and surrounding landscapes.

Stop at vineyards: Discover the history of the area's winemaking by attending wine tastings at nearby vineyards.

The Val d'Aosta

Snowboarding and Skiing

World-class skiing and snowboarding can be found at Val d'Aosta, a well-known winter sports resort tucked away in the Italian Alps. Val d'Aosta is a popular destination for travelers from all over the world because of its magnificent mountains, immaculate slopes, and quaint communities.

Resorts of the highest caliber:

Cervinia: This resort is well-known for its difficult slopes, off-piste riding, and amazing Matterhorn vistas.

Skiers and snowboarders with experience often choose Courmayeur because of its high-altitude skiing and opulent atmosphere.

La Thuile: This kid-friendly resort has a vibrant après-ski culture in addition to a range of slopes for all skill levels.

Gressoney-Saint-Jean: This quaint village is the location of multiple ski slopes, including the highest mountain in the Alps, Monte Rosa.

Various Terrain:

Black courses: Val d'Aosta has tough black courses with steep slopes and moguls for expert skiers and snowboarders.

Red routes: There are many fun red routes with different levels of difficulty for intermediate skiers and snowboarders.

Blue Runs: On mild blue runs, beginners can pick up new skills and hone their abilities.

Off-Piste: Discover the extensive off-piste terrain, which consists of backcountry areas, tree runs, and powder bowls.

Activities After Skiing:

Relaxation: Recuperate at opulent spas and wellness facilities.

Dining: Savor delectable regional fare at welcoming eateries and après-ski pubs.

Shopping: Look around quaint stores and boutiques to get one-of-a-kind mementos.

Nightlife: Savor the vibrant nightlife that includes live music venues, bars, and clubs.

How to Travel There:

Flying: The closest international airport to Val d'Aosta is Turin Airport.

Train: To get to the valley, take a train to Turin and then change to a regional train or bus.

Driving: Val d'Aosta and Turin are connected by the A5 motorway.

Trekking over the Alps

The Italian Alps' Val d'Aosta is a hiker's dream, complete with stunning scenery, varied terrain, and strenuous paths. Here's what to anticipate:

Beautiful Trails:

Matterhorn: Climb the renowned Matterhorn, one of the Alps' most difficult and rewarding treks.

Climb the tallest mountain in Western Europe, Mont Blanc, and take in expansive vistas of the neighboring summits.

Trains can be used to ascend the Jungfraujoch, a mountain pass that is home to breathtaking glaciers and ice caves.

Dolomites: Discover the Dolomites, a UNESCO World Heritage Site, with its angular peaks and vivid colors.

Various Terrain:

Hike atop glaciers to witness the breathtaking strength and beauty of these icy environments.

Alpine Lakes: Find glistening lakes that provide serene havens and breathtaking reflections, tucked away among towering mountains.

Forests: Take a stroll through verdant forests that are home to a variety of species and tall pine trees.

Alpine Meadows: During the summer, take a hike through vibrant alpine meadows that are dotted with wildflowers.

Levels of Difficulty:

Easy-to-moderate treks: A variety of easy-to-moderate hikes, including leisurely strolls through valleys and along lakeshores, are ideal for novices.

Difficult paths: The Alps provide a plethora of difficult hiking paths with high altitude conditions, complex terrain, and steep ascents for seasoned hikers.

How to Travel There:

Flying: The closest international airport to Val d'Aosta is Turin Airport.

Train: To get to the valley, take a train to Turin and then change to a regional train or bus.

Driving: Val d'Aosta and Turin are connected by the A5 motorway.

Extra Advice:

Plan Ahead: Look into certain hikes, lodging choices, and local transportation.

Examine the Weather: Before starting a hike, check the forecast because the weather in the Alps can be erratic.

Bring the necessary equipment: Wear proper clothes, good hiking boots, a hat, sunscreen, and lots of water.

Respect Nature: To preserve the delicate alpine ecosystem, adhere to the Leave No Trace philosophy.

Riding in the Mountains

Val d'Aosta is a mountain biker's dream come true because of its varied terrain, difficult trails, and stunning surroundings. Here's what to anticipate:

World-Class Pathways:

Cervinia: Take advantage of the Matterhorn's downhill runs, which offer routes for cyclists of all skill levels.

Courmayeur: Take advantage of the vast network of trails within the Mont Blanc massif, which span from easy ascents to challenging descents.

La Thuile: Wander through the meadows and forests of La Thuile to find hidden treasures. There are trails that provide breathtaking views of the surrounding mountains.

There are a number of trails available at the Aosta Valley Bike Park, including freeride areas, cross-country routes, and downhill rides.

Various Terrain:

Downhill: Enjoy the exhilaration of mountain riding on challenging descents with steep inclines and difficult terrain.

Cross-Country: Experience the wide range of cross-country trails in the area, which are appropriate for riders of all skill levels.

Enduro: For a demanding and satisfying experience, combine cross-country and downhill components.

E-bike routes offer the convenience of assisted pedaling, which makes it simpler to explore the extensive landscapes of the region.

How to Travel There:

Flying: The closest international airport to Val d'Aosta is Turin Airport.

Train: To get to the valley, take a train to Turin and then change to a regional train or bus.

Driving: Val d'Aosta and Turin are connected by the A5 motorway.

Extra Advice:

Hire a Bike: Val d'Aosta has a number of rental bike businesses that provide a range of bikes to meet your needs.

Examine Trail Conditions: Trail conditions should be monitored, particularly in the spring and fall when weather can have an impact.

Put on the Right Equipment: Put on a helmet, safety gear, and relaxed riding attire.

Respect the environment by not upsetting wildlife and by adhering to trail etiquette.

Maggiore Lake

Sailing and Boating

For those who enjoy sailing and boating, Lake Maggiore, a charming lake sandwiched between Italy and Switzerland, provides a calm and dreamy environment. A fantastic getaway from the bustle of the city, Lake Maggiore offers gorgeous landscapes, crystal-clear waters, and quaint lakeside towns.

Options for Boating:

Motorboats: Take a motorboat rental and go at your own speed across the lake's undiscovered bays, islands, and quaint settlements.

Sailboats: Take in the stunning sights and mild breezes of Lake Maggiore as you sail with excitement.

Kayaks and canoes: Take pleasure in a solitary and serene experience as you paddle across the placid lake waters.

Well-liked Locations:

Explore the enchanted Borromean Islands, which include Isola Bella, Isola Madre, and Isola dei Pescatori. Each island has its special features and breathtaking gardens.

Stresa: Discover the quaint town on the lake, known for its exquisite villas, lovely gardens, and lively atmosphere.

Explore the charming communities of Cannero Riviera, which are tucked away along the lake's western edge.

Intra: With its bustling shoreline and ancient center, Intra is the largest town on Lake Maggiore. Take in the vibrant ambiance of this town.

Price:

The type of boat, length of hire, and extra services can all affect the cost of sailing and boating in Lake Maggiore. The general cost breakdown is as follows:

Motorboat Rentals: Depending on the size and power of the boat, daily rental prices usually range from €100 to €500 or more.

Sailboat Rentals: Depending on the size and kind of sailboat, daily rental prices might range from €200 to €1000 or more.

Kayaks and canoes: Hourly or daily rental prices for kayaks and canoes typically range from €10 to €50 or more, making them more reasonably priced.

Extra Advice:

Check the Weather: Before heading out on the lake, keep an eye on the weather forecast because things can change suddenly.

Wear Appropriate Clothes: Because the weather can be unpredictable, wear layers of clothing and pack a waterproof jacket.

Think About a Guided trip: If you're new to sailing or boating, think about signing up for a guided trip to pick the brains of knowledgeable experts.

Island hopping

Situated between Italy and Switzerland, Lake Maggiore presents a great island hopping opportunity. The lake's jewels are the three charming islets known as the Borromean Islands, which are a must-see for tourists.

Bella Isle:

Gardens: Isola Bella, a botanical wonderland with an array of exotic plants, flowers, and sculptures, is well-known for its tiered gardens.

Palace: Discover the sumptuous Borromeo Palace, which is furnished with ancient furniture, magnificent murals, and breathtaking lake vistas.

The Madre Island:

Botanical Gardens: Explore an extensive assortment of rare plants and trees, such as enormous sequoias, magnolias, and azaleas.

Peacock Island: Take in the stunning ambiance created by the free-roaming peacocks that adorn the island.

The Island of Fishermen:

quaint hamlet: This little island is home to a quaint fishing hamlet with brightly colored homes, winding walkways, and quaint eateries.

Fresh Seafood: Savor delectable seafood meals made with fresh lake ingredients at the neighborhood eateries.

How to Travel There:

Boat cruises: From Stresa, a quaint village on Lake Maggiore's shoreline, regular boat cruises leave. Usually, the trips make stops at each of the three Borromean Islands.

Renting a private boat allows you to tour the islands at your own speed and provides a more individualized experience.

Extra Advice:

Plan Your Visit: It is advised to reserve your boat tour or private boat rental in advance of your visit to the Borromean Islands, as they can get congested during the busiest travel season.

Wear comfy Shoes: Because the islands are hilly, walking around the gardens and palaces will require wearing comfy shoes.

Bring a Camera: The Borromean Islands provide breathtaking photo ops, so don't forget to pack your camera to document the scenery's splendor.

Aquatic Sports

A vast array of water activities are available for fans of all ages and ability levels at Lake Maggiore, which is tucked away between Italy and Switzerland. Lake Maggiore is a water sports enthusiast's dream come true because of its pristine waters, breathtaking scenery, and wide range of activities.

Well-liked Water Sports:

Sail: Take in the stunning views of the surrounding mountains and the mild breeze as you glide across the lake's surface on a sailboat.

Using a windsurf board, you may harness the wind's strength to soar across the water.

Experience the exhilaration of kitesurfing by using a kite to soar through the air and across the ocean.

Kayaking and canoeing: Take a tranquil and personal trip in a canoe or kayak as you discover secret coves and remote beaches.

Stand-Up Paddleboarding (SUP): Take in the peace and breathtaking surroundings as you glide across the water on a paddleboard.

Wakeboarding and Waterskiing: Enjoy the thrill of wakeboarding or waterskiing while being hauled behind a boat and making jumps and tricks.

Where Can I Engage in Water Sports?

Stresa: Boat rentals, sailing schools, and windsurfing courses are just a few of the water sports activities available in the quaint village of Stresa.

Discover the Borromean Islands: Go kayaking, snorkeling, and swimming on the islands of Isola Bella, Isola Madre, and Isola dei Pescatori.

Cannero Riviera: With its serene waters and breathtaking surroundings, this charming village on the lake's western bank is a favorite destination for those who enjoy water sports.

Price:

Lake Maggiore water activities can range in price based on the type of activity, length of time, and equipment rental. The general cost breakdown is as follows:

Boat Rentals: The daily rental price of a sailboat, motorboat, canoe, or kayak can be as high as €500.

Lessons for sailing and windsurfing: Private instruction may be more expensive than group instruction, which normally costs between €50 and €100 per hour.

74

Wakeboarding and Waterskiing: Instructors can charge between €50 and €100 per hour or more for their services.

How to Travel There:

Train: Travel to Stresa or Cannero Riviera by train from the Porta Nuova station in Turin.

Automobile: Take a drive to Cannero Riviera or Stresa, both of which are conveniently located.

Extra Advice:

Verify the Weather: Before participating in any water sports, keep an eye on the forecast because the weather might change suddenly.

Wear Appropriate Clothes: Pack a hat and sunscreen, and dress in loose, quickly-drying clothing.

Think About a Guided Tour: If you're new to a certain water sport, you might want to sign up for a guided tour so you can pick the brains of knowledgeable instructors.

Chapter 4.Intercultural Perspectives

Piedmontese Food

Area-Specific Interests

Agnolotti del plin

Traditional Piedmontese pasta dish agnolotti del Plin is distinguished by its little, triangular form and delicate filling. While the filling can vary but normally consists of a combination of meat (mainly pork, veal, and beef), herbs, spices, and cheese, the pasta is usually produced using flour, eggs, and water. Usually, a meat-based sauce, like ragù or brown butter sauce, is served with the agnolotti.

Cost: Depending on the restaurant and the particular ingredients used, the price of an Agnolotti del Plin may vary. Still, most people in Piedmont agree that it's a fairly priced main course option.

Bonet

Bonet: Rich and creamy custard pudding, bonet is a traditional Piedmontese delicacy. Eggs, sugar, milk, chocolate, and amaretti cookies are the usual ingredients. The custard is frequently served with a dollop of whipped cream or a sprinkling of cocoa powder after being baked in a water bath until it sets.

Cost: In Piedmont, bonet is typically regarded as an inexpensive dessert choice. Depending on the establishment and the portion size, the price may change.

Bicerin

Bicerin: A layered drink composed with espresso, chocolate, and cream, bicerin is a typical Piedmontese beverage. Poured into a glass, first comes a layer of rich, thick chocolate, then comes a coating of whipped cream. Together, the tastes produce a rich and luscious pleasure.

Cost: Bicerin is usually regarded as a reasonably priced beverage, though the price may differ based on the establishment.

Amatriciana Bucatini

Bucinati all'amatriciana: Bucatini all'amatriciana, a traditional Roman pasta dish, consists of thick, spaghetti-like pasta combined with a tasty sauce consisting of tomatoes, onion, pecorino cheese, and guanciale (cured pork cheek). Usually having a deep and gratifying flavor, the sauce is peppery and slightly acidic.

Cost: Depending on the restaurant and the caliber of the ingredients used, the price of Bucatini all'amatriciana can change. Still, in Italy, it's often seen as a fairly priced main course alternative.

Cuisine Celebrations

Due to its rich culinary history, Piedmont holds a number of food festivals all year long to highlight the diversity of the region's cuisine and celebrate local delicacies. These are a few of the most well-liked culinary festivals:

The Bianco Tartufo Festival:

When and Where: The white truffle is a highly sought-after delicacy in the Langhe region, and this esteemed festival honors it. It usually happens in Alba between October and December.

Cost: Although admission to the festival is free, there may be fees for food, wine tastings, and other events.

How to Get There: Alba can be found roughly 31 miles (50 kilometers) south of Turin. It is accessible by automobile, bus, or train.

Salone del Gusto:

When & Where: Every two years, Turin hosts this worldwide wine and culinary exhibition. Products from all around the world are displayed, with an emphasis on local specialties and sustainable food production.

Cost: The Salone del Gusto usually has an admission charge, however the precise amount fluctuates from year to year.

How to Get There: Turin is a large Piedmont city that is conveniently reachable by automobile, bus, or train.

El Bue Grasso Fiesta:

When and Where: This yearly Turin fair honors the custom of ox rearing. It includes rides, food vendors, entertainment, and a competition for the biggest ox.

Cost: Although food and other activities may incur a fee, the Fiera del Bue Grasso is a free event.

How to Get There: Turin is a large Piedmont city that is conveniently reachable by automobile, bus, or train.

Other Food Festivals:

Festa della Birra: A beer festival showcasing regional and foreign craft brews that takes place in multiple places across Piedmont.

Sagra del Fungo Porcino: Usually celebrated in the fall, this event honors porcini mushrooms.

Sagra del Tartufo Nero: A celebration of black truffles celebrated in several Piedmont localities.

Festivals and Music

Concerts of Classical Music

Piedmont has a thriving classical music scene because of its rich cultural background. You can take in concerts by internationally recognized orchestras and musicians all year long at esteemed locations across the area.

Well-liked Performance Locations:

The large opera house of Turin, the Teatro Regio, is well-known for both its outstanding performances and acoustics.

The state-of-the-art Auditorium Giovanni Agnelli in Turin is the site of numerous classical music concerts.

Asti's historic theater, Teatro Alfieri, hosts a wide range of cultural events, such as concerts of classical music.

Novara's stunning Teatro Coccia is renowned for both its exquisite setting and top-notch productions.

When and Where:

Piedmont hosts concerts of classical music all year round, with the spring and fall months being especially active. For precise dates and timings, visit the websites of the various locations or travel agencies.

Price:

The cost of tickets for Piedmont classical music events might change according on the artists, the location, and the nature of the event. Tickets typically range in price from cheap to expensive.

How to Travel There:

Turin: The largest selection of classical music concerts may be found in Turin, the cultural center of Piedmont. Turin is conveniently accessible by car, bus, or rail.

Asti: Concerts including classical music are among the many cultural activities held in this quaint city.

There are chances to see classical music concerts in Novara, another city with a booming cultural scene.

Extra Advice:

Examine Concert timetables: Check the timetables of specific venues or travel agencies to organize your trip to take advantage of classical music concerts.

Purchase Tickets in Advance: It's advised to purchase your tickets in advance for popular performances because they tend to sell out quickly.

Dress Respectfully: Although formal wear isn't always necessary, it's usually welcomed for concerts featuring classical music.

Jazz Events

Piedmont draws music enthusiasts from all over the world to its several jazz festivals, which are held annually amid the region's thriving cultural landscape. The following are a few of the area's most renowned jazz festivals:

Jazz Festival in Torino:

When and Where: Every year, the Torino Jazz Festival takes place in Turin and brings together a wide range of Italian and international jazz performers. Usually, the celebration happens in the spring or summer.

Cost: The cost of tickets varies according on the particular performances and locations.

How to Get There: Turin is a large Piedmont city that is conveniently reachable by automobile, bus, or train.

Alba Jazz Festival:

When and Where: Alba, the global center for white truffle production, is the venue for this quaint celebration. Jazz music from the past and present is combined in the Alba Jazz Festival.

Cost: The cost of tickets varies according on the particular performances and locations.

How to Get There: Alba can be found roughly 31 miles (50 kilometers) south of Turin. It is accessible by automobile, bus, or train.

Jazz Festival in Vercelli:

When and Where: The medieval city of Vercelli is the venue for this celebration of jazz music. There are many different performances at the Vercelli Jazz Festival, ranging from modern fusion to traditional jazz.

Cost: The cost of tickets varies according to the particular performances and locations.

How to Get There: About 80 kilometers (50 miles) to the east of Turin is Vercelli. It is accessible by bus or rail.

Other Jazz Festivals

Novara Jazz Festival: This festival, which is held in Novara, has a wide range of jazz performers on its roster.

The Asti Jazz Festival is a smaller-scale event that highlights jazz musicians from the area. It takes place in the city of Asti.

How to Go:

Examine Festival Websites: For comprehensive details on dates, locations, and ticket costs, go to the websites of the particular jazz festivals in which you are interested.

Purchase Tickets in Advance: It's advised to purchase your tickets in advance for popular jazz festivals because they tend to sell out quickly.

Arrange Your Travel: Make sure to reserve your lodging and transportation in advance if you're going to a jazz festival in Piedmont.

Chapter 5.Useful Information

How to Go to and From Piedmont

How to Go Piedmont

Aircraft

Airports:

Piedmont's nearest major airport is Turin International Airport (TRN), which is situated around 20 kilometers (12 miles) north of the city center. It acts as the main entry point into the area.

Another choice is Genoa Cristoforo Colombo Airport (GOA), which is situated on the coast of Ligurian. Despite being a little further away from Piedmont, it provides more flight alternatives, particularly from foreign locations.

Well-liked Paths:

From Europe: Direct flights are available to Turin and Genoa from major European cities including Paris, London, Frankfurt, and Zurich.

From the US: Although there aren't any direct flights to Turin or Genoa from the US, there are usually connections available via significant hubs in Europe.

Terminals:

Turin International Airport features a single terminal that houses baggage claim, security, and check-in services.

The Genoa Cristoforo Colombo Airport has two terminals: Terminal 1 serves both local and international travel, while Terminal 2 caters mostly to low-cost carriers.

Price:

The cost of a flight to Piedmont can vary greatly based on the airline, the destination, the dates of travel, and demand. To get the greatest bargains, it is advised to examine the costs offered by various airlines and book your travel in advance.

Extra Advice:

Verify Baggage Restrictions: Learn about the costs and limitations on luggage that your airline may impose.

Think About Purchasing Travel Insurance: To safeguard yourself against unforeseen circumstances like flight cancellations or misplaced luggage, buy travel insurance.

Reserve Your Accommodation Ahead of Time: Piedmont's well-known tourist attractions, such as Turin, Alba, and Asti, can get busy, particularly during the busiest times of the year. Reserve your lodging well in advance to guarantee a spot.

Train

Train Itineraries:

Piedmont has excellent rail connections, with main train hubs located in Milan, Turin, and Genoa. Here are a few well-liked paths to think about:

Piedmont's capital, Turin, serves as a significant rail hub connecting the region to other cities in Italy and Europe.

Milan: Another large city, Milan has good train links to Piedmont, including high-speed trains that take about an hour to get to Turin.

Situated on the Ligurian coast, Genoa provides picturesque train rides that take travelers through the Italian Riviera and ultimately arrive in Piedmont.

Paris: Direct high-speed rail service from Paris to Turin makes Piedmont easily accessible for visitors from France.

Terminals:

Turin Porta Nuova is the city's principal train station, handling both local and foreign trains.

Milan's principal train station, Milano Centrale, provides access to other important Italian and European cities.

The principal train station in Genoa, Piazza Principe, provides connections to Piedmont and other locations.

Price:

Train travel costs to Piedmont can change based on the itinerary, time of departure, and kind of ticket. Generally speaking, saving money on tickets can be achieved by buying them in advance. To compare prices and locate the best offers, take into account using online booking services or the official websites of national train companies.

Extra Advice:

Reserve Seats: It's advised to book seats in advance on popular routes, particularly during periods of high travel demand.

Think About Rail Passes: If you intend to travel throughout Italy a lot, you might want to think about getting a rail pass, which can save you a lot of money on train tickets.

Verify Baggage Restrictions: Recognize any taxes or limitations on luggage that the railway operator may apply.

Automobile

Paths:

From France: Lyon, France, and Turin, Italy are connected by the A6 freeway. This route goes through the quaint town of Chambéry and provides picturesque views of the Alps.

From Switzerland: Geneva, Switzerland, and Turin, Italy are connected by the A1 motorway. This path offers breathtaking views of the mountains as it winds through the breathtaking Swiss Alps.

From Italy: The A1 freeway, which hugs the western edge of the Po Valley, can take you directly to Piedmont if you're already in the country.

Terminals:

Turin: The A6 freeway is the primary route that leads to Turin.

Milan: A handy route along the Po Valley leads from Milan to Turin via the A1 road.

Genoa: The Ligurian Riviera is crossed by the A7 road, which runs from Genoa to Turin.

Price:

The distance traveled, the price of fuel, and any tolls encountered along the route all affect how much it will cost to drive to Piedmont. Here are a few ballpark figures:

Cost of Fuel: The price of fuel varies throughout Italy, however a liter of gasoline should cost you between €1.50 and €2.00.

Tolls: Be ready to pay tolls along the way as there are various toll roads throughout Italy.

Vehicle Rental: Depending on the kind of vehicle and company, daily rental costs for a car might cost anywhere from €30 to €100 or more.

Extra Advice:

Examine Road Conditions: Be sure to verify the state of the roads and any potential traffic hiccups before you leave.

Plan Your Route: To plan your route and determine how long it will take, use a GPS or mapping app.

Think About Purchasing a Highway Vignette: You might need to do so if you intend to drive on Italian motorways.

Respect speed limits: Keep in mind that there may be steep fines for exceeding the posted speed limit.

Bus

Routes for buses:

Long-distance bus services connecting Piedmont to major cities in Italy and other European nations are provided by several bus companies. These are a few well-traveled paths:

Piedmont's capital, Turin, is directly served by several bus companies.

Milan is a large city in northern Italy. Turin and other Piedmontese towns may be reached by bus from Milan regularly.

Situated on the coast of Ligurian wine, Genoa provides beautiful bus tours to Piedmont.

Paris: Direct bus routes connect Paris and Turin for visitors from France.

Bus Terminals:

Turin: Porta Nuova, which is next to the train station, is the city's primary bus terminal.

Milan: Lampugnano and Porta Garibaldi are two of the city's bus terminals.

Genoa: Piazza Principe, which is next to the train station, is the city's primary bus terminal.

Price:

Bus prices to Piedmont might change according to the operator, the route, and the season. When it comes to travel, buses are typically less expensive than trains or airplanes. By comparing bus operators' fares, you might locate costs that are competitive.

Extra Advice:

Purchase Tickets in Advance: It is advised to purchase your bus tickets in advance to guarantee availability, particularly during periods of high travel demand.

Verify Baggage Restrictions: Recognize any taxes or limitations on luggage that the bus company may have.

Think About Travel Time: When organizing your vacation, keep in mind that bus travel can take longer than travel by rail or airplane.

Savor the Scenery: As you travel through Piedmont, bus travel gives you the chance to take in the beautiful scenery.

Navigating Piedmont

Train

Taking the Train to Explore Piedmont: A Practical and Beautiful Choice

Train Itineraries:

Piedmont has excellent rail access, with a network of trains servicing the region's major cities and towns. Here are a few important paths:

Turin-Milan: Piedmont's capital, Turin, is connected to Milan, one of Italy's largest cities, by high-speed rail.

Turin-Genoa: Take in breathtaking train rides that connect Turin and Genoa along the Ligurian coast.

Turin-Alba: Take a train to Alba, a quaint town famous for its white truffles, and explore the Langhe wine area.

Turin-Asti: Take a trip to Asti, a city renowned for its historical landmarks and sparkling wines.

Terminals:

Turin Porta Nuova is the city's principal train station, handling both local and foreign trains.

Milan's principal train station, Milano Centrale, provides access to other important Italian and European cities.

The principal train station in Genoa, Piazza Principe, provides connections to Piedmont and other locations.

Price:

Piedmont train prices might change according to the route, time of departure, and kind of ticket. Generally speaking, saving money on tickets can be achieved by buying them in advance. To compare prices and locate the best offers, take into account using online booking services or the official websites of national train companies.

Extra Advice:

Reserve Seats: It's advised to book seats in advance on popular routes, particularly during periods of high travel demand.

Think About Rail Passes: A rail pass might save you a lot of money on train tickets if you intend to travel around Piedmont or Italy extensively.

Verify Baggage Restrictions: Recognize any taxes or limitations on luggage that the railway operator may apply.

Discovering Piedmont's stunning scenery and quaint towns can be done in a simple and picturesque manner by rail. For both inhabitants and visitors, trains are a popular option because of its well-connected railway network.

Bus

Routes for buses:

Piedmont boasts an extensive bus system that links the region's main cities, towns, and villages. Here are a few important bus routes:

Turin-Milan: Regular bus routes provide a practical and reasonably priced means of transportation between Turin and Milan.

Turin-Genoa: Take in beautiful bus rides that connect Turin and Genoa along the Ligurian coast.

Turin-Alba: Take a bus to Alba, a quaint town famous for its white truffles, and explore the Langhe wine area.

Turin-Asti: Take a trip to Asti, a city renowned for its historical landmarks and sparkling wines.

Bus Terminals:

Turin Porta Nuova: Adjacent to the train station, this is the city's principal bus terminal.

Milano Lampugnano: A significant bus terminal in Milan that connects to several Piedmont destinations.

The principal bus terminal in Genoa, Piazza Principe, provides connections to Piedmont and other areas.

Price:

Piedmont bus fares might change based on the operator, the route, and the distance covered. When it comes to transport, buses are typically less expensive than cars or trains. By comparing bus operators' fares, you might locate competitive costs.

Extra Advice:

Purchase Tickets in Advance: It is advised to purchase your bus tickets in advance to guarantee availability, particularly during periods of high travel demand.

Verify Baggage Restrictions: Recognize any taxes or limitations on luggage that the bus company may have.

Think About Travel Time: When organizing your schedule, keep in mind that bus trips may take longer than those by rail or automobile.

Automobile

Rent a Car:

Hiring a car allows you to easily travel Piedmont at your speed and find undiscovered treasures off the usual route. In Piedmont, numerous domestic and foreign car rental agencies provide a range of automobiles to fit your requirements and price range.

Paths:

Highway Routes: Turin and Milan are connected by the A1 motorway, which provides a handy route via the Po Valley. The A6 freeway crosses the Alps to link Turin with Lyon, France.

Routes with Views: For a more picturesque trip, have a look at the meandering roads that wind through the Langhe and Monferrato districts, which are well-known for their picturesque villages and vineyards.

Terminals:

Major Piedmont train and airport terminals, like Turin International Airport and Turin Porta Nuova station, are frequently home to car rental agencies. Additionally, there are places to rent a car in well-known tourist attractions in the area.

Price:

Piedmont car rental prices might change based on the type of vehicle, the rental duration, the rental operator, and the season. In general, renting a smaller car is less expensive than renting a larger car or a premium model. By contrasting offers from various rental firms, you can locate competitive rates.

Extra Advice:

Verify Traffic Conditions: Pay attention to the flow of traffic, particularly during periods of high travel demand.

Plan Your Route: To plan your route and determine how long it will take, use a GPS or mapping app.

Think About Tolls: Be ready to pay fees as several Piedmont highways have tolls.

Respect Speed Limits: To prevent penalties and moving infractions, abide by the posted speed limit.

Savor the Scenery: You can take your time and enjoy Piedmont's breathtaking scenery as you travel through the area's quaint villages and landscapes.

cyclizing

Riding a Bike in Piedmont: A Viewful Experience

Routes for Cycling:

Piedmont has an extensive network of bike paths suitable for cyclists of all skill levels. Here are a few well-liked choices:

Langhe & Monferrato: Take a leisurely bike or take on a strenuous climb as you explore the vineyards and rolling hills of these charming districts.

Barolo Wine Route: Travel through picturesque villages and vineyards as you meander through the Barolo wine area.

Explore the breathtaking scenery of the Sesia Valley by following the paths that meander through meadows, woodlands, and mountain passes.

Lake Maggiore: Savor leisurely rides along the lake's edge while admiring the stunning vistas of the Italian Riviera and the Alps.

Terminals for Cycling:

Although Piedmont doesn't have specific cycling terminals, large towns, and tourist attractions do have bike rental and repair businesses.

Price:

Bike Rental: Depending on the kind of bike, the length of the rental, and the location, the price of renting a bike in Piedmont varies. A basic bike rental should cost you between €15 and €30 per day on average.

Guided Tours: Bike rental, a guide, and a support vehicle are frequently included in guided tours, should you prefer a guided cycling experience. Guided excursions might cost anywhere between €50 and €100 per person per day.

Extra Advice:

Plan Your Route: Look at bicycle routes ahead of time and select ones based on your interests and degree of fitness.

Verify Road Conditions: Pay attention to traffic and road conditions, particularly in congested regions.

Put on the Right Apparel: Put on bicycle gloves, a helmet, and loose-fitting clothes.

Bring the necessities: a map or GPS gadget, water, food, and a repair kit.

Savor the Scenery: Stop and take in the stunning views of the surrounding vineyards and sceneries.

Accommodation

opulent hotels

Menaggio's Grand Hotel Victoria & Regina

Grand Hotel Victoria & Regina, which is situated on Lake Como's edge, provides a sumptuous and remarkable experience. This venerable hotel offers luxurious lodging, faultless service, and stunning views of the surrounding mountains and ocean.

Price:

The Grand Hotel Victoria & Regina's rates change according to the time of year, the kind of room, and the facilities. It's crucial to remember that because this is a luxury hotel, rates are typically higher than those of more affordable choices.

How to Travel There:

Train: Travel from Milan to Como via train, and then change to a bus or ferry to Menaggio.

Car: Take a car to Menaggio from Milan or other surrounding cities. There are numerous parking lots close to the hotel.

Viareggio's Grand Hotel Royal e Excelsior

Situated on the charming Viareggio coastline in Italy, the Grand Hotel Royal e Excelsior provides an opulent and remarkable experience. This venerable hotel offers exquisite lodging, faultless service, and breathtaking views of the sea.

Price:

The Grand Hotel Royal e Excelsior's rates change according to the time of year, the kind of accommodation, and the facilities. It's crucial to remember that because this is a luxury hotel, rates are typically higher than those of more affordable choices.

How to Travel There:

Train: Travel to Viareggio by train from Florence or Pisa.

By car: Take the A12 motorway from Florence or Pisa.

Aircraft: Arrive at Pisa International Airport, from where you can take a bus or rail to Viareggio.

Turin's Hotel de la Ville

The opulent and sophisticated Hotel de la Ville is situated in the center of Turin, Italy. This old hotel offers superb service, well-furnished rooms, and a great location.

Price:

The time of year, kind of room, and facilities all affect how much it costs to stay at Hotel de la Ville. It's crucial to remember that because this is a luxury hotel, rates are typically higher than those of more affordable choices.

How to Travel There:

Train: The hotel is only a short stroll from Turin Porta Nuova station.

Car: The Hotel de la Ville is well situated in the heart of the city, close to the main thoroughfares and highways.

Airport: The distance between the hotel and Turin International Airport is about 20 kilometers. To get to the hotel, you can use a shuttle, cab, or public transit.

Affordable hotels

Alba's Hotel Italia

Nestled in the quaint town of Alba, Italy, Hotel Italia provides cozy lodgings and an ideal location for discovering the area's wineries and delectable cuisine.

Price:

The season, kind of accommodation, and facilities all affect how much a stay at Hotel Italia costs. However, in comparison to the upscale hotels in the vicinity, it's usually seen as a more affordable choice.

How to Travel There:

Train: From major Italian towns like Turin and Milan, Alba is easily accessible by train.

Car: Traveling by car to Alba is also a practical choice, as the town is connected to other regions of Italy by several important highways.

Bus: From neighboring cities and towns, bus services are offered to Alba.

Hotel Cavour in Asti

Albergo Cavour, which is centrally located in Asti, Italy, provides a cozy and reasonably priced place to stay while visiting this quaint city and the nearby vineyards.

Price:

The time of year, kind of room, and amenities all affect how much it costs to stay at Albergo Cavour. However, in comparison to the upscale hotels in the vicinity, it's usually seen as a more affordable choice.

How to Travel There:

Train: Major Italian towns like Turin and Milan have direct train connections to Asti.

Car: Considering that Asti is accessible by multiple major highways, driving there is also convenient.

Bus: Nearby towns and cities offer bus services to Asti.

Piemonte Hotel in Alessandria

Hotel Piemonte is ideally situated for touring the area's vineyards, castles, and quaint villages. It is situated in the ancient center of Alessandria, Italy.

Price:

The time of year, kind of room, and facilities all affect how much it costs to stay at Hotel Piemonte. However, in comparison to the upscale hotels in the vicinity, it's usually seen as a more affordable choice.

How to Travel There:

Train: Turin and Milan, two of the largest Italian cities, have direct train connections to Alessandria.

Car: There are numerous main highways that connect Alexandria to the city, making driving there a simple option.

Bus: From neighboring towns and cities, bus services are offered to Alessandria.

Cuneo's Hotel Roma

Nestled in the charming town of Cuneo, Italy, Hotel Roma provides cozy lodgings and an ideal starting point for discovering the Langhe wine region.

Price:

The time of year, kind of room, and facilities all affect how much it costs to stay at Hotel Roma. However, in comparison to the upscale hotels in the vicinity, it's usually seen as a more affordable choice.

How to Travel There:

Train: Major Italian towns like Turin and Milan have direct train connections to Cuneo, making it well-connected by rail.

Car: Numerous main highways connect Cuneo to the town, making driving there quite convenient.

Bus: From surrounding towns and cities, bus services are offered to Cuneo.

Etiquette and Safety

Regional Traditions and Protocols

Piedmont is a region in northern Italy with a distinct blend of cultural traditions, well-known for its breathtaking vistas, mouthwatering cuisine, and extensive history. The following are important traditions and manners to be mindful of:

Salutations and Welcomes:

Shake hands firmly: In Piedmont, a firm handshake is the standard greeting.

Titles: Unless they specifically request differently, address individuals by their titles (e.g., Signor, Signora, Dottore).

Introductions: People usually use their full names in formal introductions.

Social Protocol:

Punctuality: In Piedmontese society, timeliness is highly valued.

Hospitality: In Piedmont, being hospitable is highly regarded. Even as a guest, extend an invitation to share food or beverages with others.

Respect for Elders: Be mindful of elders' rights to be addressed with proper titles and refrain from cutting them off when they are speaking.

Dining Protocol:

When dining, Italians hold a knife in their right hand and a fork in their left.

Bread: Usually, bread is set out on a little plate on the table.

Spaghetti: It's acceptable to twirl spaghetti around a fork.

Leaving Food: Leaving a modest amount of food on your plate to signify that you were satisfied is considered courteous.

Business Protocols:

Professional apparel: Wear business casual or smart casual apparel to project professionalism.

Being on time is important while attending meetings and appointments.

Present-Giving: Bringing a little present to a social event or business meeting is a nice sign of thanks, however it is not required.

Sensitivity to Culture:

Acquire Basic Phrases: Establishing rapport can be greatly aided by knowing a few fundamental Italian phrases.

Respect Local customs: Pay attention to the traditions and customs of the area.

Steer Clear of Loud Conversations: Steer clear of loud conversations in public, especially when people are eating.

Safety Advice

Although Piedmont is a usually safe place to vacation, it's a good idea to take steps to make sure you have a fun and safe trip. The following safety advice should be remembered:

Individual Security:

Remain Alert: Pay attention to your surroundings and avoid going for long walks in remote areas, particularly after dark.

Treasures: Preserve your treasures and refrain from putting them on public display.

Public Transit: Make use of reliable services and use caution while accepting rides from strangers.

Scams: Be on the lookout for con games like pickpocketing and overcharging for products and services.

Safety and Health:

Vaccinations: Make sure you have received all the shots that are advised for visitors to Italy.

Food Safety: Take care when drinking tap water and eating raw food, particularly in rural regions.

Sun Protection: Wear sunglasses, a hat, and sunscreen to protect yourself from the sun.

Medical Assistance: Learn the locations of the closest clinics and hospitals so that you are prepared for any situation.

Travelers' Insurance:

Invest in Travel Insurance: To cover unforeseen medical costs, trip cancellations, or misplaced luggage, think about investing in travel insurance.

Extra Advice:

Learn Some Basic Italian words: Being able to converse with locals and get around will be made easier if you know a few basic Italian words.

Respect Local Customs: To prevent misunderstandings, pay attention to local etiquette and customs.

Emergency Contacts: Always have your local embassy or consulate's number ready for emergencies.

helpful websites and phone numbers for visitors visiting Piedmont

Websites for tourism:

Piedmont Region Travel Association:

- http://www.visitpiemonte.com/

Tourist Information for Turin:

- https://www.turismotorino.org/en

Tourism in Alba can be found at

- https://piedmonttravelguide.com/tour-destination/alba

Visit Asti Tourism for more information.

Transport:

- www.trenitalia.com/en.html is the website for Trenitalia.

- **Italotreno**: https://www.italotreno.com/en

- Visit BlaBlaCar at https://www.blablacar.com.

- Visit FlixBus at https://www.flixbus.com/.

Accommodation:

Reservation.com:

- https://www.reservation.com/

- **Bookings.com**: https://www.bookings.com/

- Visit AirBnB.com to book a room.

Contacts for Emergencies:

- **The emergency number in Italian**: 112

- **Police Carabinieri**: 112

- **Department of Fire**: 115

- 118 ambulances

U.S. Rome is home to the US Embassy:

- https://it.usembassy.gov/embassy-consulates/rome/

- https://www.gov.uk/world/organisations/british-embassy-rome is the address of the British Embassy in Rome.

Additional Helpful Details:

Information for Italian Travelers:

- https://www.enit.it/en

- https://www.xe.com/currencyconverter/ is the currency converter.

Temperature Prediction:

- https://www.meteo.it/

Use this link to translate languages: translate.google.com

Bonus 1: Essential Italian Phrases for Your Piedmont Trip

Make communication a breeze with these common Italian phrases, perfect for travelers in Piedmont:

- Greetings & Basics:

  - Hello / Goodbye - Ciao / Arrivederci

  - Please / Thank you - Per favore / Grazie

  - Excuse me / Sorry - Mi scusi / Mi dispiace

  - Yes / No - Sì / No

- Dining Out:

  - I would like... - Vorrei...

  - The check, please - Il conto, per favore

  - Do you have vegetarian options? - Avete opzioni vegetariane?

  - Water / Wine - Acqua / Vino

- Transportation:

  - Where is the train station? - Dov'è la stazione?

  - How much does it cost? - Quanto costa?

  - Can I buy a ticket here? - Posso comprare un biglietto qui?

- Directions & Assistance:

  - Where is... - Dov'è...

  - Can you help me? - Può aiutarmi?

  - I need a doctor - Ho bisogno di un dottore

- Shopping:

  - How much is this? - Quanto costa questo?

  - Do you accept credit cards? - Accettate carte di credito?

  - Can I try this on? - Posso provarlo?

Bonus 2: Expert Photography Tips for Stunning Shots in Piedmont

Capture Piedmont's beauty with these photography tips from the pros:

1. Golden Hour is Key: The soft, warm light just after sunrise or before sunset highlights Piedmont's landscapes beautifully.

2. Use Leading Lines: Use the region's scenic paths, rows of vineyards, or architectural features to lead the viewer's eye through your photo.

3. Capture Local Life: Include people in your shots—locals at markets, artisans at work, or chefs in their element. This adds authenticity and charm.

4. Frame with Nature: Use natural elements like tree branches or vineyard rows to frame iconic landmarks and landscapes for more depth.

5. Play with Reflections: Lakes and rivers offer stunning reflections, especially in the early morning or calm afternoons.

6. Try Different Angles: Don't be afraid to crouch low or shoot from above to capture unique perspectives, especially of historical landmarks.

7. Know When to Use HDR: For high-contrast scenes (bright skies and shaded ground), HDR mode balances exposure and brings out details.

8. Pack Light & Stay Ready: Bring versatile lenses, spare batteries, and memory cards. A lightweight kit keeps you mobile and ready for spontaneous shots.

Greetings, Reader

I sincerely hope that this book has encouraged you to travel to Piedmont in Italy, a magical place. I loved every minute of your adventure through its exquisite cuisine, rich cultural heritage, and stunning surroundings.

As a writer of travel guides, your commendable evaluations and input are priceless. They inspire me to keep producing interesting and educational content to help visitors in the future get the most out of their time in Piedmont. Your encouraging remarks give me more motivation to travel to new places and tell others about what I see.

I took my time and used a lot of resources to write and research this book to make sure the content is current and correct. Your evaluations assist me in figuring out what appeals to readers and how to make my writing better.

You're not only assisting me by sharing your ideas and experiences, but you're also assisting a growing community of travellers looking for genuine and customized travel advice. Your glowing testimonials may encourage others to start their own Piedmont travels and cultivate a passion for this stunning area.

We appreciate your help and your participation in our journey. I'm interested in hearing your opinions and going on additional trips with you in the future.

From the heart,

Gladys J. Carron

Made in the USA
Columbia, SC
18 December 2024

49898011R00063